PENNSYLVANIA

The Keystone State

BY
JOHN HAMILTON

Abdo & Daughters
An imprint of Abdo Publishing | abdopublishing.com

abdopublishing.com

Published by ABDO Publishing, a division of ABDO, PO Box 398166, Minneapolis, Minnesota 55439. Copyright © 2017 by Abdo Consulting Group, Inc. International copyrights reserved in all countries. No part of this book may be reproduced in any form without written permission from the publisher. ABDO & Daughters™ is a trademark and logo of ABDO Publishing.

Printed in the United States of America, North Mankato, Minnesota.
062016
092016

Editor: Sue Hamilton   **Contributing Editor:** Bridget O'Brien
Graphic Design: Sue Hamilton
Cover Art Direction: Candice Keimig   **Cover Photo Selection:** Neil Klinepier
Cover Photo: iStock
Interior Images: Alamy, AP, Architect of the Capitol, Benjamin West, Explore PA History, Getty, Granger Collection, Gunter Küchler, Historical Society of Pennsylvania, History in Full Color-Restoration/Colorization, iStock, Jimmy Emerson, John Hamilton, Johnstown Flood Museum, Library of Congress, Mile High Maps, Minden Pictures, National Portrait Gallery, New York Public Library, Pennsylvania Dept of Conservation & Natural Resources, Paul Kanagie, Philadelphia Eagles, Philadelphia Flyers, Philadelphia Phillies, Philadelphia Union, Pittsburgh Penguins, Pittsburgh Steelers, The Hershey Company, The State Museum of Pennsylvania-Archeology, ThinkStock, University of Pennsylvania, Villanova University, & Wikimedia.

Statistics: *State and City Populations*, U.S. Census Bureau, July 1, 2015 estimates; *Land and Water Area*, U.S. Census Bureau, 2010 Census, MAF/TIGER database; *State Temperature Extremes*, NOAA National Climatic Data Center; *Climatology and Average Annual Precipitation*, NOAA National Climatic Data Center, 1980-2015 statewide averages; *State Highest and Lowest Points*, NOAA National Geodetic Survey.

Websites: To learn more about the United States, visit booklinks.abdopublishing.com. These links are routinely monitored and updated to provide the most current information available.

Cataloging-in-Publication Data

Names: Hamilton, John, 1959- author.
Title: Pennsylvania / by John Hamilton.
Description: Minneapolis, MN : Abdo Publishing, [2017] | Series: The United
    States of America | Includes index.
Identifiers: LCCN 2015957737 | ISBN 9781680783407 (lib. bdg.) |
    ISBN 9781680774443 (ebook)
Subjects: LCSH: Pennsylvania--Juvenile literature.
Classification: DDC 974.8--dc23
LC record available at http://lccn.loc.gov/2015957737

CONTENTS

THE KEYSTONE STATE

When Quaker William Penn founded Pennsylvania in 1681, his dream was to create a land where people could live together in peace. He wanted the government to be fair to its citizens. Most of all, he cherished freedom of religion.

Today, Pennsylvania is home to almost 13 million people. It is a state made powerful by its fertile farmland, its forests, its industrial resources, and its immigrant heritage. Pennsylvania has some of the most recognizable symbols in the world, from the Liberty Bell and Philly cheesesteak, to Hershey's Kisses and the Amish horse and buggy.

A keystone is the topmost, wedge-shaped piece of a stone arch. It holds the other pieces of the structure together, much like Pennsylvania held the original 13 American colonies together with its rich resources and central location. That is why Pennsylvania is nicknamed "The Keystone State."

The Pennsylvania Amish of Lancaster County are America's oldest Amish settlement. They live a plain lifestyle, even in modern times.

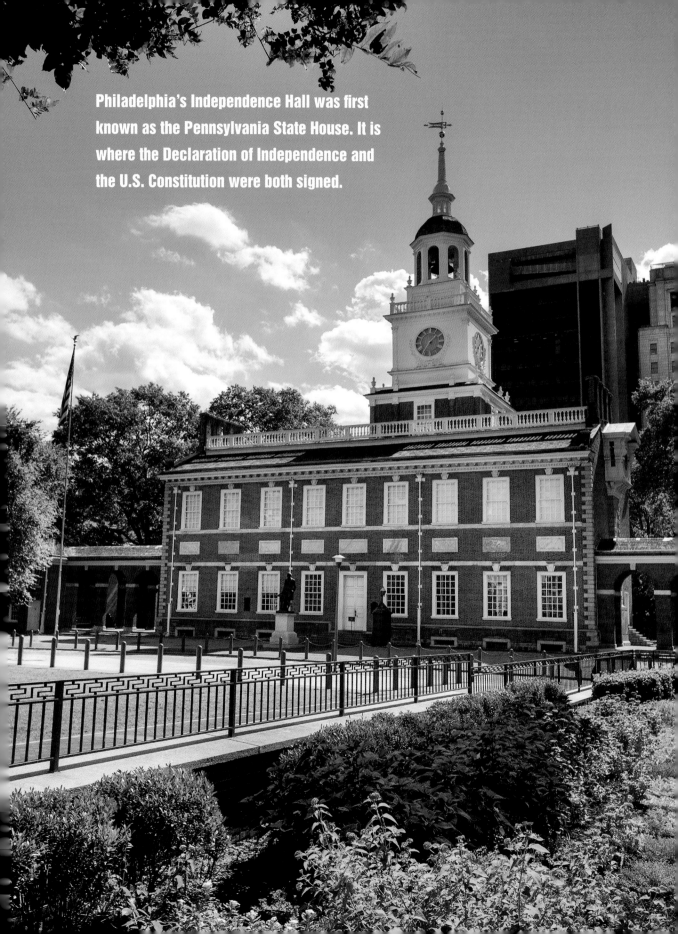

Philadelphia's Independence Hall was first known as the Pennsylvania State House. It is where the Declaration of Independence and the U.S. Constitution were both signed.

QUICK FACTS

Name: Pennsylvania is Latin for "Penn's Woods." The state was named after English Admiral Sir William Penn, the father of the colony's founder, William Penn.

State Capital: Harrisburg, population 49,081

Date of Statehood: December 12, 1787 (2nd state)

Population: 12,802,503 (6th-most populous state)

Area (Total Land and Water): 46,054 square miles (119,279 sq km), 33rd-largest state

Largest City: Philadelphia, population 1,567,442

Nickname: The Keystone State

Motto: Virtue, Liberty, and Independence

State Bird: Ruffed Grouse

State Flower: Mountain Laurel

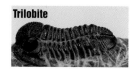
Trilobite

State Fossil: *Phacops rana* (trilobite)

State Tree: Hemlock

Hemlock

State Song: "Pennsylvania"

Highest Point: Mount Davis, 3,213 feet (979 m)

Lowest Point: Delaware River, 0 feet (0 m)

Mount Davis

Average July High Temperature: 82°F (28°C)

Record High Temperature: 111°F (44°C), in Phoenixville on July 10, 1936

Delaware River

Average January Low Temperature: 18°F (-8°C)

Record Low Temperature: -42°F (-41°C), in Smethport on January 5, 1904

James Buchanan

Average Annual Precipitation: 44 inches (112 cm)

U.S. Presidents Born in Pennsylvania: James Buchanan (1791-1868)

Number of U.S. Senators: 2

Number of U.S. Representatives: 18

U.S. Postal Service Abbreviation: PA

GEOGRAPHY

Pennsylvania is in the Mid-Atlantic region, in the northeastern part of the United States. Shaped roughly like a rectangle, it is the 33rd-largest state. It covers 46,054 square miles (119,279 sq km). Pennsylvania is the only one of the original 13 American colonies that doesn't border the Atlantic Ocean.

In the extreme southeastern corner of Pennsylvania is the Atlantic Coastal Plain region. It is a narrow strip of flat land that follows the Delaware River. The city of Philadelphia is in this region.

West and north of the Atlantic Coastal Plain is the Piedmont Plateau. It occupies a large part of southeastern Pennsylvania. It is mostly flat, but there are some rolling hills. The fertile soil makes this region excellent for agriculture. Lancaster County, with its many Amish farms, is in the Piedmont Plateau.

Much of the Piedmont Plateau is used for farming.

Pennsylvania's total land and water area is 46,054 square miles (119,279 sq km). It is the 33rd-largest state. The state capital is Harrisburg.

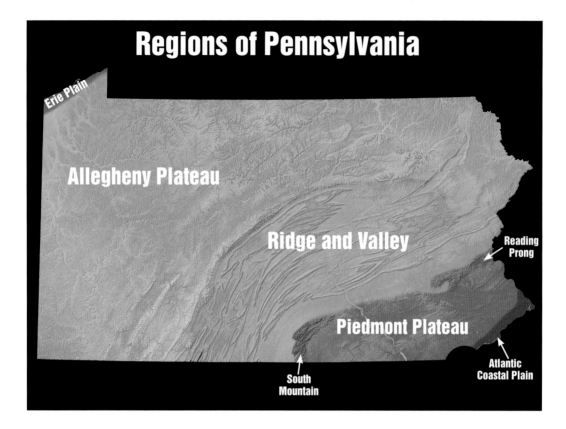

The Appalachian Mountains run through most of Pennsylvania. In the east-central part of the state are the low, forested mountains of the Reading Prong region. In the southern part of the state is the South Mountain region. It is the northern tip of the Blue Ridge Mountains.

The Ridge and Valley region includes many long, parallel ridges with valleys between them, as if a giant comb has been dragged diagonally across the landscape. The hills are forested and rugged. A number of the valleys support farming.

There are many rugged, forested mountains in the Allegheny Plateau. The Pocono and Allegheny Mountains are in this region. In the southwest is Mount Davis, the highest point in Pennsylvania. It rises in elevation to 3,213 feet (979 m).

The Delaware River cuts through the Appalachian Mountains, creating a water gap between the states of New Jersey and Pennsylvania.

In the very northwestern part of the state is a narrow strip of flat, fertile land called the Erie Plain. It borders Lake Erie, one of the Great Lakes.

Three major rivers flow through Pennsylvania. The Delaware River forms the border between Pennsylvania and New Jersey and part of New York. The Ohio River is in western Pennsylvania. The Susquehanna River flows southward through the middle of the state.

CLIMATE AND
WEATHER

Most of Pennsylvania has a continental climate. There are four distinct seasons, with warm, humid summers and cold winters. However, there is much variation between the state's many regions. In the northwest, it is colder and snowier. The southeast has warmer temperatures, with more humidity. Also, the mountains are usually cooler because of their elevation.

Statewide, the average July high temperature is 82°F (28°C). The record high occurred on July 10, 1936, in Phoenixville, when the thermometer soared to 111°F (44°C).

Lightning flashes across the sky on a hot June night in Downingtown, Pennsylvania.

A man works to clear his walkway and car after a snowstorm dumped up to three feet (.9 m) of snow on Camp Hill, Pennsylvania.

In winter, Pennsylvania's average January low temperature statewide is 18°F (-8°C). The record low temperature occurred on January 5, 1904, in the town of Smethport. That day, the mercury sank to a teeth-chattering -42°F (-41°C).

Pennsylvania averages 44 inches (112 cm) of precipitation annually. There is more snow in the mountain areas. Also, in winter, the area next to Lake Erie can sometimes receive 100 inches (254 cm) or more of lake-effect snow. In the southeast, in the Philadelphia area, there is less rain and milder temperatures.

CLIMATE AND WEATHER

PLANTS AND ANIMALS

Mountain Laurel

The word Pennsylvania means "Penn's woods." When the state's founder, William Penn, first arrived in the late 1600s, the land was almost completely forested. During the next 250 years, more than three-quarters of the woods were cut down to make room for farmland. In recent decades, much of the farmland has been abandoned, and forests have grown in their place. Today, 59 percent of Pennsylvania is forested. That is about 17 million acres (6.9 million ha).

Pennsylvania has many different kinds of trees and shrubs, thanks to its mix of mountains, valleys, and plains. The state's northern forests include beech, birch, pine, and maple. Also found in the north are hemlock, the official state tree. In the south there are oak, poplar, hickory, cherry, walnut, and elm trees. In Pennsylvania's mountains are many blackberry, raspberry, and elderberry bushes.

Flowers grow throughout Pennsylvania, from mountain forests to valley meadows. They include azaleas, rhododendrons, and honeysuckles. The state flower is the mountain laurel. Found in mountainous areas, they produce delicate white and pink petals that bloom in the spring.

Blackberries

Raspberries

Elderberries

Ricketts Glen State Park is in northeastern Pennsylvania. It is known for its old-growth trees and more than 20 waterfalls.

Black Bears

Pennsylvania has 66 species of wild mammals roaming the state's forests and valleys. Creatures commonly spotted include white-tailed deer, black bears, rabbits, gray and red squirrels, elk, raccoons, foxes, spotted skunks, bats, river otters, and beavers.

There are 414 species of wild birds in Pennsylvania. They include wild turkeys, bluebirds, robins, cardinals, peregrine falcons, osprey, herons, Canada geese, loons, screech owls, and many kinds of ducks. The official state bird is the ruffed grouse.

Ruffed Grouse

There are dozens of species of fish swimming in Pennsylvania's many lakes, streams, and rivers. Brown trout, rainbow trout, brook trout, steelhead, muskellunge, northern pike, yellow perch, and white bass are found in cooler waters. Fish that prefer warmer waters include largemouth bass, walleye, channel catfish, crappie, sauger, sunfish, bluegill, and striped bass.

Many kinds of reptiles and amphibians thrive in Pennsylvania. Common frogs include bullfrogs, northern leopard frogs, and spring peepers. Green salamanders, broadhead skinks, and eastern American toads are also commonly seen.

There are several species of snakes in the state. Most are harmless, but some are venomous. They include eastern timber rattlesnakes, northern copperheads, and Massasauga rattlesnakes. Like all snakes, they are vital to the state's ecosystems. They eat mice, voles, and rats.

Timber rattlesnakes may be found under rocky ledges in Pennsylvania.

HISTORY

About 15,000 years ago, as the last of the Ice Age glaciers finally melted, the first humans migrated to the Pennsylvania area. These Paleo-Indians were nomads who hunted the many animals in Pennsylvania's forests.

Centuries later, the people organized and formed groups, called tribes. By the 1600s, they included the Lenni-Lenape, Susquehannock, Shawnee, and Iroquois people. The Lenni-Lenape were the most numerous. They were often called the Delaware Indians because they lived in villages along the Delaware River.

John Smith

Henry Hudson

John Smith from England explored the Pennsylvania area in 1608.

Henry Hudson, working for the Dutch, explored Pennsylvania in 1609.

In 1608, John Smith from England explored the Pennsylvania area. He was followed in 1609 by Henry Hudson. He was also from England, but worked for the Dutch government.

After Hudson's explorations, the Dutch claimed the Pennsylvania area. However, the first Europeans to settle there came from Sweden. They arrived in 1643 and set up trading posts as part of the colony of New Sweden. They traded for valuable furs with local Native Americans.

The Dutch and Sweden battled over the land. The Dutch eventually won, but their victory didn't last long. In 1664, England defeated the Dutch and permanently took control of the resource-rich area.

William Penn negotiated a treaty with Pennsylvania's Native Americans in 1682.

Tragically, contact with Europeans caused many Native Americans to catch deadly diseases such as smallpox and measles. Warfare further weakened the tribes. Some fought one another as they competed to sell furs to French and English traders.

In 1681, England's King Charles II gave a large piece of land in North America to William Penn. The land was named Pennsylvania, which combined the Penn family name with the Latin word for woods, *sylvania*.

William Penn was a member of the Religious Society of Friends. Often called Quakers, the Christian group refused to wage war, hated slavery, and believed in social justice. They were often persecuted and jailed in England.

In his new colony, William Penn wanted to create a place where people could live together in peace. He wrote a state constitution called the *Frame of Government of Pennsylvania*. Citizens were given the right to own land, worship as they pleased, and granted other freedoms.

Many English Quakers came to live in Pennsylvania. Some settled in the new city of Philadelphia, which was founded in 1682. The colony also attracted other immigrants, from many different religions, who sought freedom. A large number of the newcomers came from Ireland and Germany.

By the time of the Revolutionary War (1775-1783), when the 13 American colonies fought for independence from Great Britain, Philadelphia had grown into a powerful city. The First and Second Continental Congresses met in Philadelphia. The Declaration of Independence was signed on July 4, 1776, in the Pennsylvania State House, now called Independence Hall. After the war was won, the United States Constitution was also signed in Independence Hall, in 1787.

Benjamin Franklin

Thomas Jefferson

George Washington

On December 12, 1787, after ratifying the United States Constitution, Pennsylvania became the second state in the Union.

On December 12, 1787, Pennsylvania became the second state to approve the Constitution and join the Union (Delaware was the first). It is officially named the Commonwealth of Pennsylvania. "Commonwealth" in this case has the same meaning as "state."

Philadelphia served as the nation's capital for several years, until it was moved to Washington, DC, in 1800. Pennsylvania continued to be very important. The state's factories made goods that the young nation's people needed.

In the years before the Civil War (1861-1865), Pennsylvania became a refuge for African Americans fleeing slavery in the South. During the war, the state remained in the Union. It sent more than 350,000 soldiers and sailors to fight against the pro-slavery Southern Confederacy. Many bloody battles were fought in Pennsylvania, including the Battle of Gettysburg in 1863.

Some of the Civil War's deadliest battles occurred in Pennsylvania. The Battle of Gettysburg, which took place from July 1 to 3, 1863, was the bloodiest single battle ever fought on American soil.

After the Civil War, Pennsylvania became a powerful manufacturing state. Companies used its many natural resources, including coal and lumber. Pennsylvania was a leading producer of iron and steel. Many mills, foundries,

Molds are filled with steel at a Pittsburgh plant.

railroads, and shipyards sprang up. During World War I (1914-1918) and World War II (1939-1945), Pennsylvania provided huge amounts of steel, coal, and ships to the war effort. It also supplied thousands of troops, many of whom lost their lives defending the United States.

Pennsylvania suffered a decline in its economy from the 1960s until the mid-1980s. It became known as part of the "Rust Belt." Competition from foreign countries hurt the state's heavy industries, including steel and machinery manufacturing.

To revive its economy, in recent decades Pennsylvania has diversified its businesses. It now relies more on high-technology industries and companies that perform services such as health care, finance, and insurance.

DID YOU KNOW?

• The Liberty Bell is a symbol of freedom known throughout the world. Starting in the early 1750s, it rang from the bell tower of Philadelphia's State House (known today as Independence Hall). It may have been rung when the Declaration of Independence was first read aloud to the public on July 8, 1776. The bell is made of bronze (70 percent copper, 25 percent tin, with small amounts of lead, gold, and silver), and weighs 2,085 pounds (946 kg). The inspiring text at the top of the bell reads, "Proclaim LIBERTY throughout all the Land unto all the inhabitants thereof." The bell became a powerful symbol before the Civil War for those wishing to abolish slavery, which is when it first became known as the Liberty Bell. No one knows when it developed its famous crack. Today, it is preserved in the Liberty Bell Center in Philadelphia's Independence National Historical Park.

• Except for the Liberty Bell, Philly cheesesteaks may be Philadelphia's most beloved symbol. They are made of thin-sliced, rib-eye steak, melted cheese, and fried onions, served on a crusty hoagie roll. To order properly, one uses the "whiz wit" system. For example, if you want a classic cheesesteak with Cheez Whiz and onions, simply say, "One whiz wit." ("One" means one cheesesteak, "whiz" means Cheez Whiz, and "wit" means "with onions.") If you don't like onions, say, "One whiz wit-out." If you prefer a different kind of cheese, substitute it for "whiz," such as "One provolone wit."

• Lancaster County, west of Philadelphia, is a rural area that is home to many Amish people. They are members of a Christian group that believe in living simply. They avoid most modern conveniences and technology. They drive horse-drawn buggies and wear plain, old-fashioned clothing. The Amish are famous for their skills as farmers, and in creating handmade crafts and furniture.

DID YOU KNOW?

PEOPLE

Benjamin Franklin (1706-1790) was a larger-than-life character who did much to help the United States in its early years. Usually dressed in plain clothing, he was a politician who helped write the Declaration of Independence and the United States Constitution, and negotiated peace with Great Britain at the end of the American Revolution. He was an author and printer, best known for his witty *Poor Richard's Almanack*. Franklin was also a scientist and inventor. He explored math, electricity, and mapmaking, and invented bifocal glasses and swim flippers. He created the first American lending library. Franklin was a firm believer in lifelong learning. As he once said, "We are all born ignorant, but one must work hard to remain stupid." Franklin was born in Boston, Massachusetts, but spent most of his adult life in Philadelphia, Pennsylvania.

Taylor Swift (1989-) is a country- and pop-music superstar. The singer-songwriter released her first professional album in 2006, when she was just 16 years old. The self-titled album was a huge hit, and in 2007 she won the Academy of Country Music Awards' Top New Female Vocalist. In 2008, she released *Fearless*, which won the Grammy Award for Album of the Year. At age 20, she was the youngest person ever to win the award. In recent years, she has released pop songs, including the smash "Shake It Off" from the 2014 album *1989*. By 2016, she had sold more than 40 million albums. She has won 10 Grammy Awards, 19 American Music Awards, and 11 Country Music Association Awards. Swift was born in Reading, Pennsylvania, but grew up in nearby Wyomissing.

Milton Hershey (1857-1945) was born on a farm near the rural Pennsylvania town of Derry Church. He learned how to make candy as a teenager. He worked as a confectioner in several cities before moving back to Pennsylvania. In 1894, he started the Hershey Chocolate Company. A few years later, he bought land near his birthplace and built an enormous chocolate factory. He used milk from nearby dairy farms to make his own recipe for fine milk chocolate. Sales took off, and the company became famous for chocolate bars and Hershey's Kisses. The town that sprang up around the factory was named for the founder. Today, Hershey, Pennsylvania, is called "The Sweetest Place on Earth."

Dr. Daniel Hale Williams (1856-1931) was an African American pioneer of cardiology. He was one of the first doctors in the world to successfully perform surgery to repair a wounded heart. In 1891, Dr. Williams founded Provident Hospital in Chicago, Illinois. It was the first hospital to be run by African Americans. It also had many African American doctors and nurses, and accepted patients of all races. Dr. Williams was born in Hollidaysburg, Pennsylvania.

Kobe Bryant (1978-) was born in Philadelphia, Pennsylvania. Growing up, he wanted to be a professional basketball player, just like his father, Joe "Jellybean" Bryant. In 1996, he was chosen as a first-round draft pick directly out of high school. He played his entire 20-year career with the National Basketball Association's Los Angeles Lakers. He retired in 2016 as one of the most successful shooting guards in NBA history, winning five NBA championships and many other honors.

CITIES

Philadelphia is the largest city in Pennsylvania. Its population is about 1,567,442. Together with its suburbs, the entire Philadelphia metropolitan area is home to more than 7 million people. Established in 1682 by William Penn (the colonial founder of Pennsylvania), the word *Philadelphia* means "brotherly love" in Greek. Today, the "City of Brotherly Love" is an economic powerhouse. Key industries include high technology, manufacturing, education, food processing, health care, and financial services. Millions of tourists visit the city each year, attracted by historical icons such as the Liberty Bell, Independence Hall, and other colonial sites protected within Independence National Historical Park. The Philadelphia Zoo was the nation's first zoo. It opened in 1874. The University of Pennsylvania was founded by Benjamin Franklin. It enrolls more than 24,000 students.

Pittsburgh is Pennsylvania's second-largest city. Its population is 304,391. It is located in the western part of the state, where the Monongahela and Allegheny Rivers merge to form the Ohio River. It is often called the "City of Bridges" because of its 446 bridges, many of them painted official Aztec gold. Founded as a frontier fort in 1758, Pittsburgh grew into an industrial giant that was the center of the steel industry, along with many other manufactured goods. Today, the steel industry is not as important. In its place, top industries now include high technology, health care, finance, education, and tourism. The Carnegie Museum of Natural History was founded in 1895 by influential businessman Andrew Carnegie. The museum has more than 22 million specimens in its collections, including dinosaur fossils.

CITIES

Harrisburg is the capital of Pennsylvania. Located in the south-central part of the state, its population is about 49,081. Established in 1718 as a trading post and to ferry people and goods across the Susquehanna River, the city was originally named Harris's Ferry. It was renamed in 1812 when it became Pennsylvania's capital. Today, the city's economy depends on high-technology firms, government, retail, and food processing. The impressive capitol dome reaches a height of 272 feet (83 m). The city is located in the fertile Susquehanna Valley. The annual Pennsylvania Farm Show is the largest indoor agricultural fair in the country. It includes almost 6,000 animals and 10,000 competitive exhibits.

The PPL Center is a multipurpose arena that opened in 2014 in downtown Allentown.

Allentown is the third-largest city in Pennsylvania. Its population is approximately 120,207. It is located in east-central Pennsylvania, north of Philadelphia, in the Lehigh Valley. Founded in 1762 by wealthy businessman and attorney William Allen, the city grew because of its busy factories. In recent decades, Allentown's economy has depended more on service industries such as retail, health care, and finance. The downtown and riverfront areas have been redeveloped to include people-friendly retail shops, restaurants, and hotels. The Allentown Art Museum, which contains more than 17,000 works of fine art, has been in the downtown area since the 1930s.

TRANSPORTATION

Early in Pennsylvania's history, Philadelphia was an important port for shipping goods such as grains. They could be floated down the Delaware River to the Atlantic Ocean, where they could be sent to other states or countries.

Today, Philadelphia is joined by the Port of Pittsburgh and the Port of Erie. The Port of Pittsburgh handles more than 35 million tons (31.8 million metric tons) of cargo each year. That makes it one of the busiest inland ports in the country.

Barges and train cars haul Pennsylvania coal.

Philadelphia International Airport is Pennsylvania's busiest airline hub.

There are 119,936 miles (193,018 km) of public roadways in Pennsylvania. Several interstate highways crisscross the state, making it easier for automobiles and trucks to cross Pennsylvania's many ridges and mountains.

There are 57 freight railroads in Pennsylvania. They travel on 5,151 miles (8,290 km) of track. Coal is the most common cargo hauled. Other items include chemicals, stone, food products, metal products, plus sand and gravel.

Pennsylvania has several large airports. They include Philadelphia International, Pittsburgh International, and Lehigh Valley International Airports. Philadelphia International is the state's busiest. It handles more than 31 million passengers each year.

TRANSPORTATION

NATURAL
RESOURCES

About 27 percent of Pennsylvania is covered by farmland. That is approximately 7.7 million acres (3.1 million ha). There are nearly 58,000 farms in the state.

Pennsylvania's most valuable crops include hay, feed corn, soybeans, wheat, tobacco, sweet corn, potatoes, pumpkins, oats, beans, and strawberries. There are also many apple orchards. Pennsylvania is the fifth-largest producer of milk in the United States.

A pumpkin farm in Pennsylvania. Pumpkins are one of the state's most valuable crops.

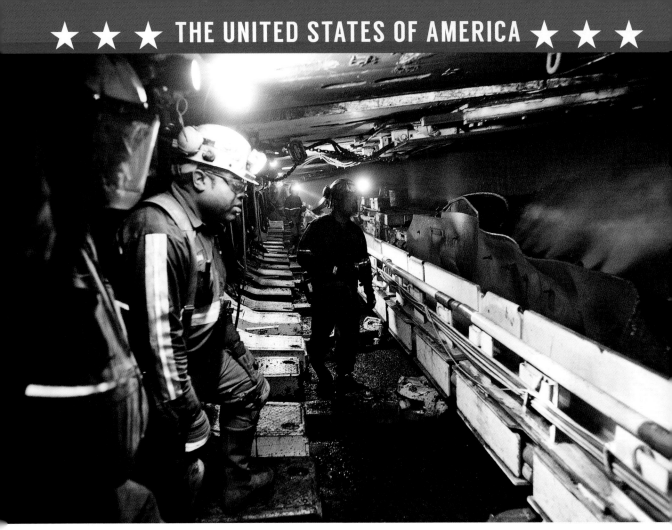

Coal miners watch a shearer scrape coal from the wall during longwall mining operations in Wind Ridge, Pennsylvania.

Pennsylvania is the fourth-largest producer of coal in the nation. The industry employs tens of thousands of workers who dig coal from the state's rich veins deep in the Earth. The burning of coal accounts for about 40 percent of Pennsylvania's electricity generation. Other materials mined in Pennsylvania include iron, limestone, oil, natural gas, plus sand and gravel.

Forestland covers about 59 percent of Pennsylvania. That is about 17 million acres (6.9 million ha). The state is the country's number-one grower of hardwood trees, including oak and hickory. The forest products industry supports more than 90,000 Pennsylvania jobs.

INDUSTRY

Early in Pennsylvania's history, agriculture was the biggest part of the state's economy. In the 20th century, coal mining and steel production turned Pennsylvania into an economic powerhouse. Today, the service industry is the state's biggest employer.

Of Pennsylvania's 6.5 million workers, more than half work in the service industry. It includes businesses such as advertising, financial services, health care, insurance, restaurants, retail stores, law, marketing, and tourism.

The Children's Hospital of Philadelphia is one of the top hospitals specializing in care for boys and girls in the United States.

The Hershey Company West facility manufactures such products as Hershey's Kisses, Hershey's Milk Chocolate Bars, and Hershey's Syrup. Milton Hershey opened the original factory in 1905. Today, that location is a popular tourist attraction called Hershey's Chocolate World.

Manufacturing remains a major part of Pennsylvania's economy. Many factories are centered around the Philadelphia and Pittsburgh areas. Important manufactured products include steel, fabricated metals, machinery, transportation equipment, food processing, clothing, glass, electronics, chemicals, paints, and paper products.

Nearly 193 million people visit Pennsylvania each year. They are drawn by the state's natural beauty and its wealth of historical treasures. Visitors spend approximately $40 billion in the state annually. Tourism supports more than 480,000 jobs.

SPORTS

Pennsylvania has many professional sports teams. The Pittsburgh Steelers and the Philadelphia Eagles play in the National Football League (NFL). The Steelers have won the Super Bowl six times, more than any other NFL team.

The Philadelphia Phillies and the Pittsburgh Pirates are Major League Baseball (MLB) teams. The Phillies have won two World Series titles. The Pirates have won five times.

The Philadelphia 76ers shoot hoops in the National Basketball Association (NBA). Commonly called "The Sixers," they have won three NBA championships.

The Philadelphia Flyers and the Pittsburgh Penguins skate in the National Hockey League. The Flyers have won two Stanley Cup championships, while the Penguins have won four times.

The Philadelphia Union is a Major League Soccer team. It played its first game in the state in 2010.

The Little League Baseball World Series (LLBWS) is held each August in South Williamsport, Pennsylvania. The first LLBWS was held in 1947. It began as a tournament for United States teams, but is now an international competition.

College sports are big in Pennsylvania, especially football and basketball. The most popular teams include those from Penn State University, the University of Pittsburgh, Temple University, La Salle University, and Villanova University.

Little League Baseball began in 1939 in Williamsport, Pennsylvania. Today, there are more than 7,000 teams worldwide. Each August, the Little League Baseball World Series is held in South Williamsport.

ENTERTAINMENT

P hiladelphia's Independence National Historical Park preserves many landmarks from the American Revolution, including the Liberty Bell and Independence Hall. The park receives more than 3.5 million visitors each year.

The Philadelphia Museum of Art has a massive collection of more than 227,000 works of art. It is also the site where boxer Rocky Balboa ran up the steps during his training in the movie *Rocky*.

Valley Forge National Historical Park preserves the site where General George Washington and the Continental Army camped during the brutal winter of 1777-1778.

The popular Philadelphia Museum of Art was built in the 1920s. Standing on a tall granite hill, the stairs and building are a well-known icon.

Punxsutawney Phil looks for his shadow on Groundhog Day.

Reenactments with hundreds of costumed volunteers are held each year near Gettysburg National Military Park, site of the pivotal Civil War battle of 1863.

Each February 2, on Groundhog Day, the people of Punxsutawney, Pennsylvania, anxiously wait to see if Punxsutawney Phil, the town's fabled groundhog, will be frightened by his shadow, signaling six more weeks of winter.

Duquesne Incline

In Pittsburgh, visitors can ride the 1800s-era Duquesne Incline cable car up Mount Washington, one of the city's many steep hills. There is an observation deck at the top overlooking the city.

TIMELINE

13,000 BC—The first Paleo-Indians migrate to the Pennsylvania area.

1600s—Native Americans living in the Pennsylvania area include the Lenni-Lenape, Susquehannock, Shawnee, and Iroquois people.

1609—Henry Hudson claims the Pennsylvania area for his Dutch employers.

1643—Settlers from Sweden begin Pennsylvania's first permanent European settlement.

1664—England gains control of the Pennsylvania area.

1681—England's King Charles II gives Pennsylvania to William Penn.

1774—The First Continental Congress meets in Philadelphia.

1775—The Second Continental Congress meets in Philadelphia.

1776—The Declaration of Independence is signed in Philadelphia.

1787—Pennsylvania ratifies the U.S. Constitution and becomes the second state to join the Union.

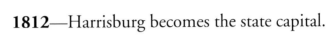

1812—Harrisburg becomes the state capital.

1859—The nation's first successful oil well is constructed near Titusville.

1863—The Battle of Gettysburg is fought during the Civil War. The Union Army wins the battle.

1889—The South Fork Dam on the Little Conemaugh River bursts. Floodwaters destroy the town of Johnstown, killing more than 2,200.

1894—Milton Hershey starts the Hershey Chocolate Company.

1979—Three Mile Island nuclear power plant accident occurs.

2009—Pittsburgh Steelers win the Super Bowl for the sixth time.

2016—The Villanova University Wildcats win the NCAA men's basketball national championship.

GLOSSARY

COAL

A hard, brown or black fossil fuel that is burned to create heat, most often at power plants that generate electricity. About 46 percent of America's electricity needs are met by burning coal.

COMMONWEALTH

A word for a government that is formed to promote the common good of the people. Pennsylvania declares itself a commonwealth, but it has the same meaning as "state."

CONFECTIONER

A person who earns a living making and selling candy and other treats.

CONSTITUTION

A set of laws that establish the rules and principles of a country or organization.

CONTINENTAL CONGRESS

The government assembled by the 13 American colonies when they revolted against British rule.

FOSSIL

The preserved remains or impression of prehistoric animals or plants in stone.

ICE AGE

An Ice Age occurs when Earth's climate causes a major growth of the polar ice caps, continental ice shelves, and glaciers. The ice sheets can be more than one mile (1.6 km) thick.

LAKE-EFFECT SNOW

Winter weather systems that cause unusually large amounts of snow to fall. The weather systems picks up moisture when they blow over large bodies of water, such as Lake Erie, and then dump snow on land that is close to shore.

PALEO-INDIANS

The first residents of Pennsylvania. Most people believe these were the ancestors of modern Native American tribes.

PIEDMONT

An Italian word that means "at the foot of the hills."

PLATEAU

A relatively flat area of high ground.

QUAKER

A member of the Religious Society of Friends. The Quakers are a Christian movement founded in 1650 by George Fox. They believe in principles of peace and tolerance.

SERVICE INDUSTRY

Businesses that do work for customers, like insurance or health care. Service industries do not normally manufacture things.

INDEX